Life in the American Co

The Real Story on the
WEAPONS
and BATTLES
of Colonial America

by Kristine Carlson Asselin

Consultant:
Dr. Samuel B. Hoff
Professor of History
Delaware State University
Dover, Delaware

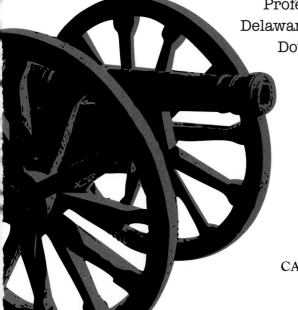

D1473494

CAPSTONE PRESS
a capstone imprint

Fact Finder Books are published by Capstone Press,
1710 Roe Crest Drive, North Mankato, Minnesota 56003.
www.capstonepub.com

Books published by Capstone Press are manufactured with paper
containing at least 10 percent post-consumer waste.

Library of Congress Cataloging-in-Publication Data
Asselin, Kristine Carlson.
  The real story on the weapons and battles of Colonial America / by Kristine Carlson Asselin.
    p. cm.—(Fact finders. Life In Colonial America)
  Includes bibliographical references and index.
  Summary: "Describes various weapons and battles of the colonial period in America"—Provided by
publisher.
  ISBN 978-1-4296-6491-2 (library binding)
  ISBN 978-1-4296-7985-5 (paperback)
  1. United States—History—Colonial period, ca. 1600-1775—Juvenile literature. 2. United States—
History, Military—To 1900—Juvenile literature. I. Title.
E188.A88 2012
973.2—dc23   2011033677

Editorial Credits
Mandy Robbins, editor; Ashlee Suker, series designer; Svetlana Zhurkin, media researcher;
    Laura Manthe, production specialist

Photo Credits
Alamy: Classic Image, 13, North Wind Picture Archives, 7, 15, 19, 23; BigStockPhoto: Aptyp_koK, 4;
Corbis: Bettmann, 21, 27; iStockphoto: Brian Swartz, 11; Library of Congress, cover (middle), 8, 25; Line
of Battle Enterprise, 29; North Wind Picture Archives, 9, 17; Shutterstock: alexkar08 (linen texture),
throughout, diless (pattern), throughout, Ev Thomas, 26, Irina Tischenko (wood board), throughout,
Michael Vigliotti, 12, photocell (wooden frame), throughout, stocksnapp, 28, Viachaslau Kraskouski
(wooden planks), throughout

Printed in the United States of America in Brainerd, Minnesota.

102011   006406BANGS12

TABLE OF CONTENTS

Chapter 1

Life in a NEW LAND

British colonists first settled in America in the late 1500s and early 1600s. They found a wild and beautiful country. But starting a new life in the wilderness was difficult. Colonists had to build shelters, find food, and meet all of life's needs. To meet these needs, colonists had to learn new skills and use tools they had never used before.

Most colonists had never fired a gun before leaving Great Britain. In their home country, hunting was a sport for wealthy landowners. Few colonists had been wealthy in Great Britain. But life in America required the use of weapons. Colonists needed to hunt if they wanted to eat. Hunting wild game was one of the few ways colonists could get food.

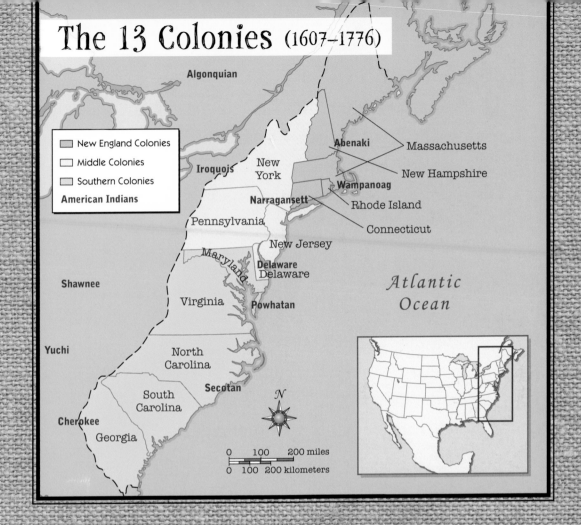

The 13 Colonies (1607–1776)

Algonquian

New England Colonies
Middle Colonies
Southern Colonies
American Indians

Iroquois

Abenaki

New York

Massachusetts

New Hampshire

Wampanoag

Narragansett

Rhode Island

Pennsylvania

Connecticut

New Jersey

Maryland

Delaware
Delaware

Shawnee

Atlantic Ocean

Virginia

Powhatan

Yuchi

North Carolina

Secotan

South Carolina

Cherokee

Georgia

N

0   100   200 miles
0 100 200 kilometers

Colonists also used guns for protection. Wild animals roamed the forests of the new world. Meeting a hungry bear without a gun was a recipe for disaster. But colonists also used guns to defend themselves from the other people who lived in America.

WHO THEY FOUGHT

Most of the first American colonists were British. But the Spanish, French, Dutch, and Swedish also had colonies in North America. The British often found themselves at odds with neighboring colonies. They battled over boundary lines and control of land and waterways. These battles often led colonists to turn their weapons on each other.

Millions of American Indians had called this land home for thousands of years. Many American Indians were helpful at first. But cultural differences between American Indians and the colonists were hard to ignore. Disagreements about religion, culture, and land often turned violent.

By the late colonial period, the colonists had carved out their own place in North America. But many colonists disliked being ruled by a country that was across the ocean from them. They wanted to create their own government. The colonists used their weapons to fight for independence.

Dutch and British settlers in Connecticuit fought over land rights.

independence—freedom from the control of other people or things

Chapter 2

WEAPONS

European colonists survived the harsh new land with help from American Indians. However, the two groups were very different. Between cultural differences and land disputes, it wasn't long before fighting broke out. Nowhere were the differences between these groups more obvious than in battle.

European colonists wore layers of thick clothing and heavy armor. American Indians wore much less clothing by comparison.

EUROPEAN ARMOR

British armor was heavy and bulky. Some men wore leather or metal armor across their chests. Metal skirts protected their legs. Helmets looked like iron pots. All this gear could weigh up to 24 pounds (11 kilograms). The colonists' heavy armor slowed them down.

Armor made it difficult for colonists to move quickly while hunting or in battle.

EUROPEAN WEAPONS

European soldiers carried heavy swords, long pikes, and guns. Swords were the most common weapons. They were used in hand-to-hand combat for slashing and stabbing.

Pikes were long poles with sharp pointed blades on the ends. They were 12 to 16 feet (4 to 5 meters) long. Pikes were used for stabbing and fighting off cavalry charges. Soldiers stood side-by-side to create a wall of spikes as their enemies charged. Eventually, bayonets replaced pikes.

Lieutenant Archelaus Fuller, describing the 1758 Battle of Ticonderoga during the French and Indian War:

"Before the regular soldiers came up, the fire began very hot. The regulars threw down their packs and fixed their bayonets; came up in order; stood and fought very courageously."

[Text has been changed for clarity.]

Colonists often used cannons to guard their settlements from an attack.

The most advanced weapons were guns. Muskets were the common guns used by most European armies. In the 1700s, bayonets were attached to the barrels of muskets to combine the two weapons.

Colonists also brought cannons from Europe. These heavy guns took up to 14 men to operate. The guns were up to 8 feet (2.4 meters) long. Cannons could blow holes in walls, attack ships, and destroy large targets.

cavalry—a unit of soldiers who fight on horseback

bayonet—a long metal blade attached to the end of a musket or rifle

AMERICAN INDIAN WEAPONS

American Indians carried light weapons so they could move quickly in battle. Bows and arrows were the most common tools. From a young age, warriors were trained to be very accurate with their bows.

The tomahawk was used in hand-to-hand combat. A tomahawk was an axe with a thin blade attached to a straight handle. Tomahawks were made in many different sizes.

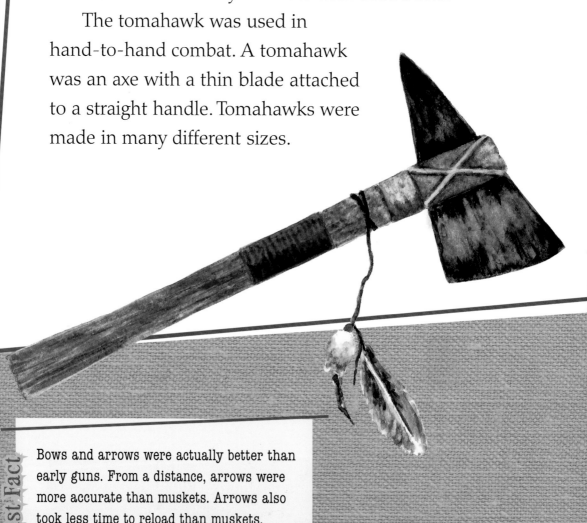

American Indians also used a long throwing spear called an atlatl. It was made of chipped stone, bone, or shell. This weapon acted like a lever. Warriors put the end of an arrow into one end of the atlatl. Then they flung the device from the other side. Using an atlatl increased the speed and distance of a flying arrow.

Without very accurate guns, most colonial combat was done at close range.

Chapter 3

BATTLE Tactics

One big difference between Europe and the colonies was that colonists didn't have a regular army. All men between the ages of 16 and 60 joined a local force called the militia. The militia would be called to action when needed. These men used the same fighting styles practiced in Europe.

Europeans had always fought battles out in the open. Their battles had to happen on open ground for their battle formations to be successful. All soldiers aimed and fired their weapons at the same time to be most effective.

The American Indian battle technique was quite different. They often sent a large war party to sneak up on a small enemy camp and strike by surprise. Another strategy was to abandon any type of organized formation. Warriors scattered and struck from behind trees. Eventually, the colonists picked up the American Indians' stealth tactics. They launched their own sneak attacks on native villages.

stealth—having the ability to move secretly

Most colonial militias did not have uniforms.
They fought in their everyday clothes.

BATTLE CRIES

American Indians entered into battle with a terrible wailing sound. This war cry distracted and scared the colonists. Soldiers often scattered and were easier to attack.

The British also made a loud noise when entering battle. But this noise was made by muskets. When American Indians first heard the sound of gunfire, they were terrified. They didn't realize the deadly force of the weapons. It was the smoke and boom of the guns that scared the American Indians.

John Smith, *The Journals of Captain John Smith*, 1608:

"Upon the discharging of our muskets they all fled and shot not an arrow. The first house we came to we set on fire, which when they perceived, they desired we would make no more spoil and they would give us half they had."

[Text has been changed for clarity.]

When it came to battle damage, Europeans caused much more devastation than the American Indians. When American Indian tribes fought each other, a small number of warriors were killed and injured. But the colonists wiped out entire native villages. American Indians were caught off guard by so much violence. With such forceful tactics, Europeans defeated more and more tribes. American Indians who survived were pushed west.

The colonists burned down an entire Pequot Indian village in 1637.

Chapter 4

Early BATTLES

PEQUOT WAR, 1634-1638

Trade with the American Indians and Europeans was an important source of income for the colonists. It also caused the first major battle between colonists and American Indians. In the early 1600s, a Pequot tribe had a village in present-day Connecticut. The village was located along the Connecticut River. The spot was a perfect place for a trading post. Whoever controlled that land would make a lot of money from traders. Massachusetts Bay colonists wanted the Pequot tribe off the land so they could control it.

The Pequots and the colonists fought over the area. Some Pequots killed a British trader after a member of their tribe was kidnapped.

During the final battle of the Pequot War, at least 600 Pequot Indians were killed in about a half hour.

The colonists struck back by burning the Pequot's crops. The Pequot people struck again, killing nine colonists and taking two girls captive. The British then joined with the Pequots' enemies, the Mohegan Indians. Together, the colonists and Mohegans burned the Pequot village to the ground. At least 600 Pequots were killed. The colonists easily took over the land. This was the first major war between colonists and American Indians. But it wasn't the last.

KING PHILIP'S WAR, 1675

The Pilgrims settled the first permanent colony in present-day Massachusetts in 1620. The colonists wouldn't have survived their first winter without help from the local Wampanoag Indians. Chief Massassoit befriended the colonists. He hoped they would help fight off his enemies, the Narragansett Indians. But the friendship between the Wampanoags and the Pilgrims only lasted 50 years.

King Philip was the son of Chief Massasoit. Philip's people had been forced off their land by the steady stream of colonists coming from Britain. He declared war in order to reclaim his land. Philip convinced many tribes to join his fight. However, other tribes sided with the colonists. Indian warriors helped the colonists kill Philip and defeat his army.

John Sassamon in a letter written to the British colonists on behalf of King Phillip, 1663:

"Last summer Philip swore that he would sell no land in 7 years time. He wants no English to trouble him before that time. He has not forgot that you agreed with him."

[Text has been changed for clarity.]

American Indians attacked settlers in their cabins in Deerfield, Massachusetts, during King Philip's War.

King Philip's War lasted one year. About 600 colonists and 3,000 American Indians were killed. The fighting destroyed communities along the east coast. The American Indians who survived moved west. Many colonists also moved to other areas. It took the New England colonies years to recover from the loss of life and property damage.

Fast Fact

King Philip's Wampanoag name was Metacom. He adopted the English name Philip.

Chapter 5

Leading Up to the AMERICAN REVOLUTION

The American colonists did not decide to break away from Great Britain all at once. Their frustration with British rule grew over many years. Certain battles helped fuel the spirit of independence.

BACON'S REBELLION, 1676

The farmers of Virginia had heard about King Philip's War in New England. Many colonists saw American Indians as a threat and wanted the government to do something about it. Nathaniel Bacon was one of them.

Governor William Berkeley knew that some American Indians were hostile to the colonists. But he wanted to keep the peace. Berkeley continued trading with peaceful tribes. Many colonists believed the governor was protecting the American Indians for his own profit.

Bacon and many of his neighbors took matters into their own hands. Bacon's army attacked a local Pamunkey tribe, even though the tribe had done nothing to provoke the colonists.

Governor Berkeley tried to reason with the colonists before he fled Jamestown.

Bacon's group then marched to Jamestown to find the governor. They chased him out of Jamestown and burned down the town.

Bacon's Rebellion is sometimes called the first fight for independence. Colonists realized they had the power to stand up to their governmental leaders.

FRENCH AND INDIAN WAR, 1754–1763

By 1754 Great Britain had settled 13 colonies in North America. France, the Netherlands, Sweden, and Spain also had North American colonies. The British government viewed these other colonies as threats to their empire.

Great Britain wanted to increase its holdings in North America. France held land on the border of what is now New York and Canada. Both countries wanted to claim part of present-day Pennsylvania. It wasn't long before tension turned to gunfire.

Both sides tried to get American Indians to join them. Most tribes sided with the French. British colonists had forced many Indians off their land. The French were more interested in setting up trading posts than settlements.

 Fast Fact

The French and Indian War has also been called the Seven Years War, even though it lasted nine years.

empire—a large territory ruled by a powerful leader

George Washington (on horse) began his military career in the French and Indian War.

The French and their American Indian allies had some successful battles. But the British completely overwhelmed them by sending large numbers of troops from Great Britain. In the end, France lost almost all of its land in North America to Great Britain.

After the French and Indian War, colonists were more experienced in organized battle. And very soon, that experience would be put to use.

ally—a person, group of people, or country that gives support to another

Chapter 6

When a Nation REVOLTS

Great Britain spent a fortune on the war against France. Since the colonies benefited from the war's success, they were expected to pay their share. The British government taxed the colonists. Many colonists were angry about paying taxes when they had not been able to vote on the decision.

The final straw came in 1773 when Britain passed the Tea Act. This law taxed tea. Most colonists drank tea every day. In protest, up to 130 men stormed three ships that had carried tea into Boston Harbor. They threw crates of tea into the water. About 340 crates of tea were destroyed. This event is known as the Boston Tea Party.

Fast Fact

Taxes were passed on games such as cards and dice. Newspapers, calendars, and court papers such as licenses and college diplomas were also taxed.

As punishment, the British government closed Boston Harbor until residents paid for the tea. Boston's local government was replaced with a council appointed by the British governor. At least 4,000 British soldiers were sent to Massachusetts to keep order among the colonists. Boston was under siege.

Colonists disguised themselves as American Indians during the Boston Tea Party.

tax—the act of collecting money from a country's citizens to help pay for running the government

siege—an attack designed to surround a place and cut it off from supplies or help

1775: THE REVOLUTION BEGINS!

Throughout the colonies, people felt their freedom was threatened. The cry for independence grew louder. Local militias prepared to fight.

Massachusetts Governor Thomas Gage suspected the colonists were planning to fight. His spies discovered a stockpile of weapons in Concord, 20 miles (32 kilometers) from Boston. The governor sent several hundred British soldiers to destroy the weapons.

Colonial spies discovered Gage's plan. Paul Revere and several others warned local colonists. On the way to Concord, the British soldiers marched into Lexington. Sixty armed colonists met them there.

At this point, someone fired the first shot of the Revolutionary War (1775-1783). No one knows who fired first, but by the time the dust settled, eight colonists were dead. With only one man wounded, the British marched on to Concord.

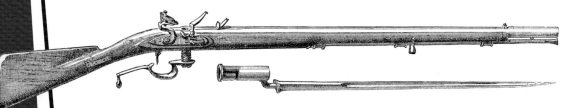

Poet Ralph Waldo Emerson called the first shot at Concord "the shot heard 'round the world" because it changed the course of history.

When they got to Concord, the weapons were gone. The British split up to search the town. As they did this, militia men from nearby towns arrived. The militia chased the British back to Boston. Many British soldiers were killed or wounded along the way.

There was no turning back from war now. Over eight years of fighting, the stealth tactics the colonists had learned from American Indians proved valuable. The colonists defeated the world's largest superpower of the time. By 1783 their last battle as British subjects was over. They were officially Americans.

GLOSSARY

ally (AL-eye)—a person, group of people, or country that gives support to another

bayonet (BAY-uh-net)—a long metal blade attached to the end of a musket or rifle

cavalry (KA-vuhl-ree)—a unit of soldiers who fight on horseback

empire (EM-pire)—a large territory that is ruled by a powerful leader

independence (in-di-PEN-duhnss)—freedom from the control of other people or things

siege (SEEJ)—an attack designed to surround a place and cut it off from supplies or help

stealth (STELTH)—the ability to move without being detected

tax (TAKS)—the act of collecting money from a country's citizens to help pay for running the government

READ MORE

Catel, Patrick. *Soldiers of the Revolutionary War.* Why We Fought, the Revolutionary War. Chicago: Heinemann Library, 2011.

Raum, Elizabeth. *The Dreadful, Smelly Colonies: The Disgusting Details about Life During Colonial America.* Disgusting History. Mankato, Minn.: Capstone Press, 2010.

Santella, Andrew. *The French and Indian War.* Cornerstones of Freedom. New York: Children's Press, 2012.

INTERNET SITES

FactHound offers a safe, fun way to find Internet sites related to this book. All of the sites on FactHound have been researched by our staff.

Here's all you do:

Visit *www.facthound.com*

Type in this code: 9781429664912

Super-cool stuff! Check out projects, games and lots more at **www.capstonekids.com**

INDEX

PRIMARY SOURCE BIBLIOGRAPHY

Page 10: Anderson, Fred. *A People's Army: Massachusetts Soldiers and Society in the Seven Years' War.* Chapel Hill, North Carolina: University of North Carolina Press, 1984.

Page 16: Smith, John. *The Journals of Captain John Smith*, 1608.

Page 20: 1663 Letter written by John Sassamon. Published by the Pilgrim Hall Museum: www.pilgrimhall.org